Peruvian
WEAVERS

Rob Waring, *Series Editor*

HEINLE
CENGAGE Learning

Australia • Brazil • Japan • Korea • Mexico • Singapore • Spain • United Kingdom • United States

Words to Know

This story is set in Peru. It happens in a village in the Andes Mountains. The village is called Chinchero [tʃiːntʃerou] and it is near the city of Cuzco [kuːskou].

A **High in the Andes.** Read the definitions. Write the number of the correct underlined word next to each item in the picture.

1. <u>Barley</u> is a plant which produces small grains used for food and drink.
2. A <u>sheep</u> is an animal that farmers often raise for wool, meat, and milk.
3. A <u>potato</u> is a white root vegetable with brown, red, or yellow skin.
4. A <u>llama</u> is an animal that people often use to carry things in the Andes.
5. A <u>farmer</u> is a person who raises animals or plants for food.

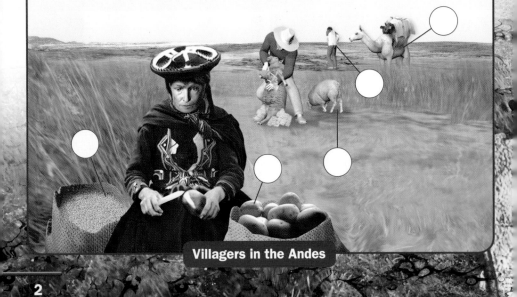

Villagers in the Andes

B **Traditional Peruvian Weaving.** Read the paragraph. Then match each word with the correct definition.

This story is about a group of women weavers in a small village. These weavers use wool, or the hair from sheep and llamas, to make cloth. They do this by crossing pieces of yarn or other material over and under one another. This process is called weaving. The weavers make blankets for their beds and shawls to wear so they can stay warm. They also sell these items and use the money to help the local economy.

1. wool _____

2. cloth _____

3. yarn _____

4. weave _____

5. blanket _____

6. shawl _____

a. a material often used for making clothing

b. sheep or llama hair

c. a warm covering for the bed

d. a thin twisted fibre made of cotton, wool, etc.

e. an article of clothing worn around the shoulders

f. make cloth by crossing pieces of yarn over and under one another

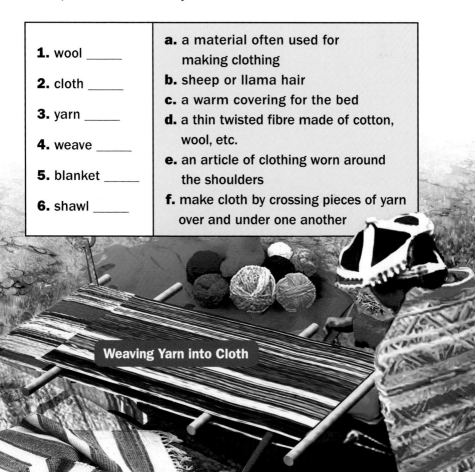

Weaving Yarn into Cloth

In a small village high in the Andes, the weaving process starts with just one sheep. First, a few people from the village, or villagers, prepare the **knife.**[1] Then, they carefully tie up the sheep so that it can't move. Finally, they use the knife to cut the sheep's winter coat of wool. After that, one of the newest and most important industries in Chinchero begins.

---

[1] **knife:** a tool used to cut things

Cutting Wool from a Sheep with a Knife

The methods they use are traditional, but these villagers really are part of something new. The wool they're collecting is for a new and different type of business in the village of Chinchero. It's for a weavers' **cooperative**[2] that the women here manage.

Every Monday and Saturday, 46 women and girls – all members of the cooperative – cut wool from their sheep and llamas. Then, they **spin**[3] the wool and work it into yarn. After that, they use the yarn to make cloth.

---

[2] **cooperative:** a business owned jointly with others
[3] **spin:** turn wool or another material into yarn

Nilda Cayanupa[4] is the leader of the Centre for Traditional **Textiles**,[5] which manages the cooperative. She explains why she helped to start the cooperative: "[Not many people] of my age in my town [were] learning to weave. So it was kind of sad that weaving was disappearing. So, because [of] that, my dream was always that the younger **generation**[6] should learn [how to weave] so the weaving won't die."

Nilda and the cooperative are working to ensure that the traditional weaving of the Andes won't disappear.

---

[4] **Nilda Cayanupa:** [nɪldə kaɪənuːpə]
[5] **textile:** general term for cloth or things people weave
[6] **generation:** people of a similar age within a society or family

Nilda grew up in the Andean **countryside,** [7] where many of the men are farmers. According to Nilda, her village produces a lot of very good foods. "Chinchero is a farming village," she says. "We are the best – I'm not saying [this] because I am from this village – but we are the best producers of potatoes, and many things like **quinoa** [8] [and] barley."

---

[7]**countryside:** land in its natural condition that is not in a town or city

[8]**quinoa:** a plant grown for food and often eaten like rice

cloth

Fact Check: True or false?

1. The women cut wool from sheep and llamas every day.

2. There are over fifty women in the cooperative.

3. In Chinchero, people grow potatoes and other food.

shawls

blankets

yarn

quinoa

potatoes

Many products are made or grown in Chinchero.

Farming has been a tradition in Chinchero for a long time. Many farmers here continue the traditions of the **Inca people**[9] who lived in the Andes for centuries.

However, the economy is changing. Farming no longer brings in enough money to support a whole family here. So, with the changes in the economy, traditional ideas are changing, too. Until now it's always been the men who have farmed. Traditionally, the women have cooked and looked after the children. They have also taken wool from the sheep and woven it into cloth. It's this weaving process that is now becoming more and more important.

---

[9]**Inca people:** South American group of people from long ago

Nilda agrees that these women weavers are becoming more important. They're becoming the main economic supporters of the family. As an example, she speaks about one woman whose husband has started helping with the sheep. She explains that this wasn't very common in the past. Until recently, the men only farmed the land and didn't help with the weaving. This is now changing because women can make a good amount of money with their weaving. Nilda says, "Today, this group of ladies can make ... not a lot of money ... but a reasonable amount of money."

Now in Chinchero, Peruvian weaving isn't just a tradition anymore. It's a way for these women to make money and live well.

Weaving has also become more important for the culture of Chinchero. It has become a way to make the textile tradition stronger and to keep a part of the past alive. One older weaver talks about how she learned how to weave: "I learned when I was in the third grade of school with very basic weaving," she says. "Today, I weave blankets, shawls, **ponchos,**[10] and prepare my own yarn."

The older women here are now teaching the younger girls. The goal is to bring back the strength of the textile tradition of the past. They want to keep the Peruvian weaving traditions alive.

---

[10] **poncho:** a piece of clothing shaped like a blanket with a hole for the head

As the young women of Chinchero learn to weave, they also learn to be **self-sufficient.**[11] They can sell the blankets and clothes that they make in their free time. "I do my weaving in my house, in the afternoons and the early morning," explains one young girl. "And [at the cooperative] on Monday and Saturday, too," she adds.

Weaving groups like the Chinchero cooperative are giving new life to the textile tradition. In the end, their cooperative may show that many **threads**[12] together are stronger than one alone.

---

[11] **self-sufficient:** financially independent; able to live without help from others
[12] **threads:** long, thin pieces of wool or cotton used in weaving; a very thin form of yarn

Infer Meaning

1. What does the writer mean by the last sentence?

2. What makes you think that?

After You Read

1. On page 4, the word 'industries' means:
   A. farming methods
   B. communities
   C. business activities
   D. ways of cutting wool

2. What is the purpose of the paragraph on page 4?
   A. To describe the industries in Chinchero.
   B. To show what happens to sheep in Chinchero.
   C. To introduce the Colombian countryside.
   D. To describe the village of Chinchero.

3. On page 7, 'it' in paragraph two refers to:
   A. cloth
   B. yarn
   C. cooperative
   D. wool

4. According to page 7, how are the villagers involved in something new?
   A. They've made a new community for weaving.
   B. They've developed a new way of collecting wool.
   C. The women are managing a new village.
   D. The wool is new and different.

5. A good heading for page 8 is:
   A. Centre for Traditional Textiles is Unsuccessful
   B. Weaving Totally Disappears from Andes
   C. A Dream to Help Traditional Weaving
   D. Weaving Has Died

6. On page 10, the word 'produces' can be replaced by:
   A. sells
   B. grows
   C. buys
   D. contains

7. Which item comes from the Andean countryside?
   A. tomatoes
   B. bread
   C. potatoes
   D. all of the above

8. How is the economy changing in Chinchero?
   A. Farming is becoming stronger.
   B. Men are starting to weave.
   C. Women are making money from weaving.
   D. Men are cooking for children.

9. Weaving is a way _____ women to support their families.
   A. to
   B. for
   C. that
   D. in

10. Recently, husbands in Chinchero have started to help with the sheep.
   A. True
   B. False
   C. Not in text

11. On page 17, 'they' in paragraph two refers to:
   A. older women
   B. girls
   C. young women
   D. families

12. On page 18, what does the young girl probably think about weaving?
   A. Weaving takes a lot of time.
   B. Weaving can only be done on Saturdays.
   C. Weaving helps her to be self-sufficient.
   D. Weaving has to be done at the cooperative.

Foods of
THE WORLD

A s part of our series on 'Foods of the World', reporter Ana Ruiz met traveller and food writer Monica Mason. Monica has just returned from South America where she was studying traditional foods of the Inca. Read on to discover what interesting facts she uncovered.

Quinoa

Q: WHY DID YOU DECIDE TO GO TO PERU?

A: My aim was to learn as much as I could about the traditional foods of the Inca people. I spent some time with families in small villages in the mountains. I wanted to see what foods they ate. I had a feeling that some of the 'modern' foods that we eat today are actually traditional foods.

Q: WHAT DID YOU LEARN?

A: I was correct. Recently, doctors have told people to eat quinoa to be healthy, but quinoa was actually often used in traditional Inca foods. It was even more common than the potato. This was because quinoa was easy to grow in dry areas near the tops of mountains. That's where a lot of the people lived.

Q WHAT ELSE DID THEY EAT?

A: The Inca ate a lot of potatoes as well, but they weren't as important as quinoa. Most people have always been able to get potatoes. However, it's only in the past twenty years that we can buy the healthier quinoa. I find that a bit strange.

Q: WHAT WAS THE MOST INTERESTING THING YOU LEARNED ABOUT THE INCA?

A: One interesting thing is that they had a method of storing potatoes for long periods of time. When the weather became very cold, they would place potatoes in the ground all night. This caused them to become very cold and hard, or 'freeze'. During the day, the Inca would put the potatoes near a hot fire. This combination of hot and cold caused the potatoes to dry out. Once they were dry, they could keep the potatoes for a long time.

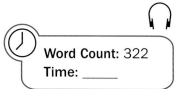

Word Count: 322
Time: _____

Vocabulary List

barley (2, 10, 11)
blanket (3, 11, 17, 18)
cloth (3, 7, 8, 11, 17, 18)
cooperative (7, 8, 10, 18)
countryside (10)
disappear (8)
farmer (2, 10, 13)
knife (4)
llama (2, 3, 7, 10)
poncho (17)
potato (2, 10, 11)
quinoa (10)
self-sufficient (18)
shawl (3, 11, 17)
sheep (2, 3, 4, 5, 7, 10, 13, 14)
spin (7)
textile (8, 17, 18)
thread (18)
weave (3, 4, 7, 8, 13, 14, 17, 18)
wool (3, 4, 5, 7, 10, 11, 13, 18)
yarn (3, 7, 11, 17, 18)